What's in this book

This book belongs to

_____

方向 The directions

学习内容 Contents

沟通 Communication

说出交通工具
Say means of transport

说出方向
Say the directions

生词 New words

★ 东	east
★ 南	south
★ 西	west
★ 北	north
★ 远	far
★ 近	near
★ 校车	school bus
★ 出租车	taxi
★ 更	even more
★ 要	will

背景介绍：
马路上，一个男孩正在向路人问路。

Post Office

School

Supermarket

公里	kilometre (km)
公共汽车	bus
电车	tram
语文	language
考试	examination

中国古代四大发明之指南针
One of the Four Great Inventions
of ancient China —— the compass

句式 Sentence patterns

坐公共汽车或电车更快。
It is faster to take the bus or the tram.

浩浩和玲玲要坐校车回家。
Hao Hao and Ling Ling will take the
school bus to go home.

跨学科学习 Project

制作指南针，并利用指南
针辨认方向
Make a compass and use it
to tell directions

参考答案：
1 Yes, I got lost in the supermarket two years ago./No, I have a good
sense of direction.
2 I asked a passer-by for directions./I called my mum on her mobile phone.
3 The boy looks worried and the woman is giving him directions.

Get ready

1 Have you ever been lost somewhere before?

2 What did you do to find your way?

3 How can you tell that the boy in the picture is lost?

读一读 Read

故事大意：
放学后，浩浩和玲玲在车站准备坐校车回家，发现一个男孩迷路了，找不到
要去考试的地方。浩浩和玲玲合力帮他找到了最快到达目的地的方式。

xiào chē
校车

"要"指即将做某一件事。如"校
车要开了。"指校车即将开出。

yào
要

School bus

参考问题和答案：

1 Where are Hao Hao and Ling Ling? What are they doing?
(They are at the school bus station. They are about to take
the school bus home.)

2 How does the boy look? What has happened? (The boy
looks worried. He has lost his way.)

浩浩和玲玲要坐校车回家。在车站，
一个男孩迷路了，向他们问路。

"你们好，请问语文中心怎么走？"
男孩问。

参考问题和答案：
1 What is the boy doing? (He is asking Hao Hao and Ling Ling for directions.)
2 Where does the boy want to go? (He wants to go to the Language Centre.)

"语文中心在东南方向，要走两公里。坐公共汽车或电车更快。"浩浩说。

"更"用于比较时，表示程度加深。
如"他比你高，比我更高。"

"这么远啊，我以为很近。我要去考试，怎么去最快？"男孩问。

"坐出租车最快。西边有一个出租车站。"玲玲说。

"直走到路口，向北转就到车站了。"
玲玲说。"谢谢你们！"男孩说。

Let's think

1 Recall the story and circle the correct answers. 提醒学生回忆故事，观察第5页和第8页。

1 男孩要去哪里?

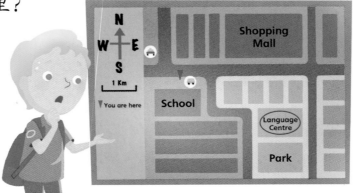

2 坐什么车去最快?

(a)

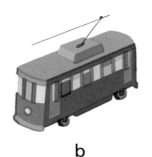

b

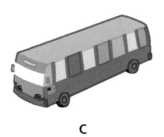

c

2 What would you do if you got lost? Tick the boxes and discuss with your friend.

参考答案:
I would ask the police for help./I would use the map to find the destinations.
老师可告诉学生，迷路时不要惊慌，除了用力所能及的办法找到方向之外，还可以打电话寻求家长或者警察的帮助。

New words

 1 Learn the new words.

延伸活动：
老师可准备本课和已学交通工具的图片，让学生看图说词，看谁回答得又快又好。此外，学生还可讨论学校的方位，并说说学校四周有什么。

电车

校车

SCHOOL BUS

出租车

更快

公共汽车

TAXI

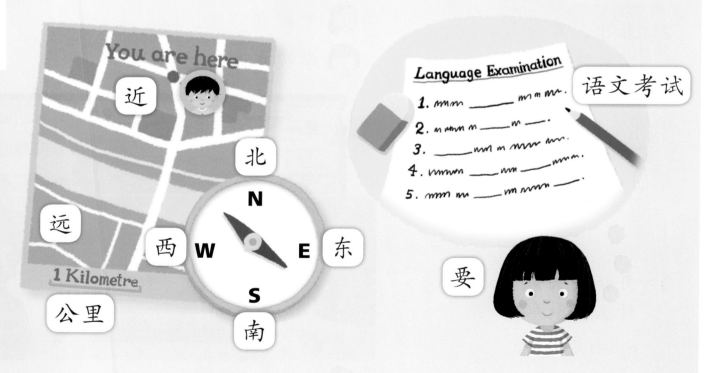

You are here

近

远

1 Kilometre

公里

北

西

东

南

N W E S

Language Examination

1.
2.
3.
4.
5.

语文考试

要

2 Say the words to your friend and ask him/her to point out the correct words above.

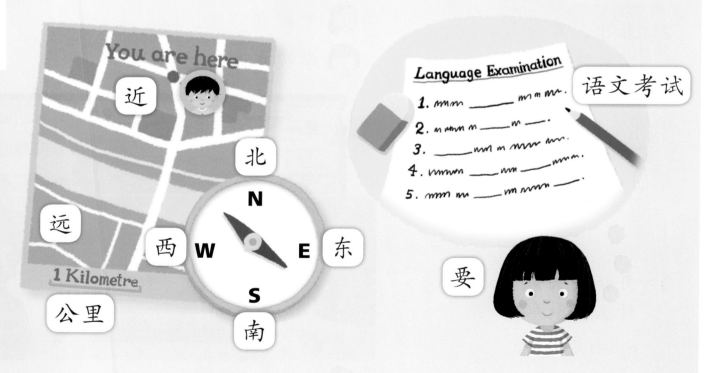

1 Listen and circle the correct letters.

1 动物园在学校的哪个方向？

a 南边

b 西边

(c) 北边

2 坐什么车去男孩家更快？

a 公共汽车

(b) 电车

c 出租车

3 男孩要去做什么？

a 打羽毛球

(b) 考试

c 看书

2 Look at the pictures. Listen to the story an

学校在哪里？

学校在西北边。

公共汽车站在哪里？

路上有汽车和校车，但是没有看到公共汽车站。

y.

 哪里可以骑自行车？

东南面的草地边可以骑自行车。

 小狗要去哪里？

 小狗要去草地上玩，很近。

3 Write the letters and say.

a 公共汽车	b 东	c 更
d 西	e 远	f 要

1

弟弟比我矮，妹妹比我__c__矮。

2

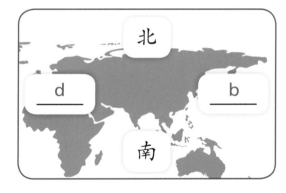

北
__d__　　__b__
南

3 我们__f__坐__a__去爷爷家。

爷爷家很__e__。

Task

全班同学可按交通方式来分类举手统计，然后按结果画图并作报告。

How do your classmates go to school every day? Make a transport survey chart and report.

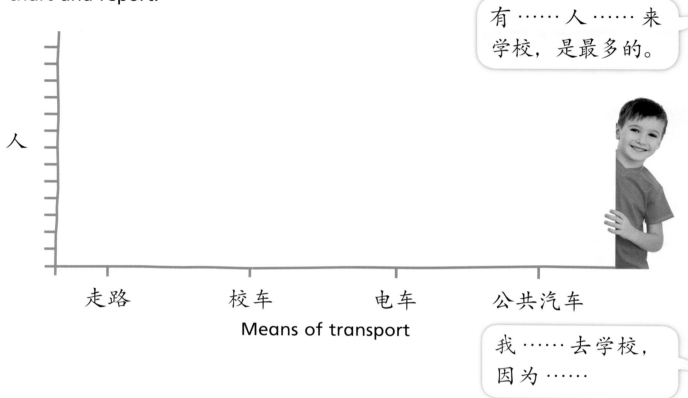

有……人……来
学校，是最多的。

人

走路　　校车　　电车　　公共汽车

Means of transport

我……去学校，
因为……

Game

Match the halves of the means of transport together and then find the correct word for each one. 提醒学生按各交通工具的特点来连线，如校车是黄色的，电车上方有电线等。

校车　　公共汽车　　电车　　出租车

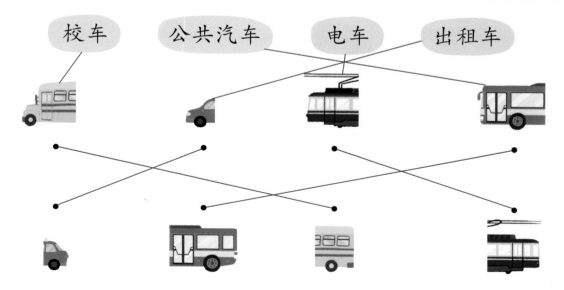

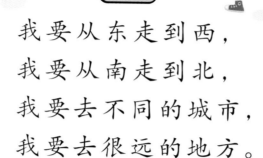

北

我要从东走到西，
我要从南走到北，
我要去不同的城市，
我要去很远的地方。

我要从西走到东，
我要从北走到南，
我要去不同的国家，
我要去更远的地方。

西

东

南

生活用语 Daily expressions

去……怎么走？
How can I get to ...?

不远。
Not far away.

写一写 Write

1 Trace and write the characters.

一 二 テ 元 元 沅 远

远

"远"和"近"有相同的
"走之底"部件。该部件
的字多与"行走"有关。

一 ナ 广 斤 近 近

近

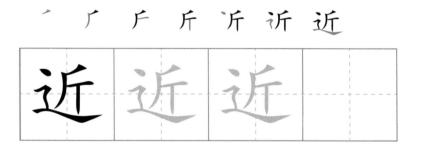

一 ナ 亓 而 西 西 覀 要 要

要

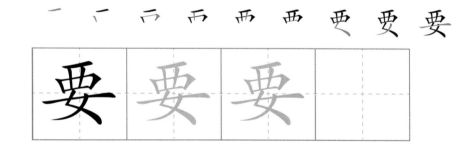

2 Write and say.

石头很 近 ，
船很 远 。

校车 要 开了，
请快点上车。

16

提醒学生同一颜色的空位表示需写同一字或词，每种颜色只配对某一个字或词。
学生做完题目后，仔细阅读该段落加深理解。

3 Fill in the blanks with the correct words. Colour the shells using the same colours.

我们
红色

远
黄色

近
绿色

天
蓝色

家人
粉色

今年夏 天 ，我和 家人 一起坐汽车去海边的城市旅行。那里在我们家的东边，很 远 ， 我们 坐车用了两个小时。城市的北边还有动物园，坐车只用二十分钟，很 近 。 我们 都玩得很开心。

拼音输入法 Pinyin input

Match the sentences to the pictures using the letters and then organize the sentences into a meaningful paragraph. Type it out.

c

b

d

a

a 大象还很喜欢玩水。它们真可爱。

b 大象的耳朵很大，鼻子很长。

c 我最喜欢的动物是大象。三岁时，我和爸爸一起去动物园看大象。

d 它喜欢吃草。

老师提醒学生分别注意四幅图的特点：小时候的"我"和爸爸；大象的体貌；大象吃草；大象玩水，然后与句子中的重要信息配对。

多元学习 Connections

1 Did you know that the compass was one of the Four Great Inventions of ancient China? Learn about it.

This compass was made up of a bronze plate and a magnetized spoon. It was used to identify directions and tell fortunes in ancient China.

This compass was used for navigation during the 11th century. The magnetized needle could move freely and point to the earth's magnetic poles.

The ancient Chinese compasses pointed to the south. Today's compasses, however, point to the north

学生两人一组，互相问答，句式尽量多元化。除了运用题目中的句式外，
还可用"……站在哪里/什么方向？""……是……站吗？"等。

2 Where are the stations? Talk about them with your friend.

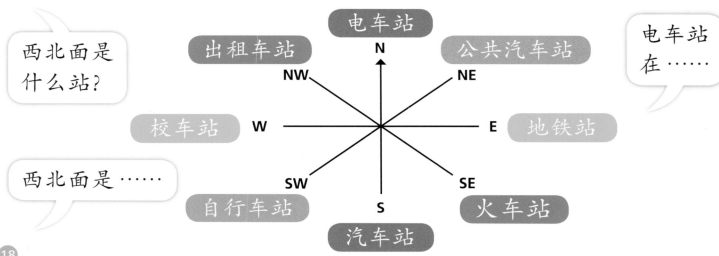

西北面是什么站？

西北面是……

电车站在……

电车站
出租车站
公共汽车站
校车站
地铁站
自行车站
汽车站
火车站

1 Make a compass.

材料：一根缝衣针、一块磁铁、一块硬币大小的圆形软木塞、一个盛有水的碗。

①

② 将缝衣针在磁铁上沿同一方向多次摩擦，注意不要来回摩擦。

③ 将摩擦好的针穿过软木塞。

④ 将穿着软木塞的缝衣针轻轻放入水中。

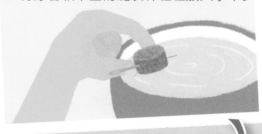

⑤ 让穿着软木塞的缝衣针浮于水面，轻轻转动。静止后，针会分别指向南和北。

Observe the sun or stars to find out which direction is north and mark on your compass!

可根据平时的经验、观察正午的太阳或者夜晚的星星来确定针的哪一头是北或南，也可用标准指南针来检验，然后用笔在软木塞上做标记以便之后使用。但要注意自制指南针的指向可能会发生偏角。

2 Use the compass to identify the positions of your home, nearby buildings and the school. Discuss with your friend.

学生可利用现有的指南针或者自制指南针，描述家与附近地点及学校的方位。

学校在……边，公共汽车站在学校的……边。

我家在城市的……面，我……上学。

我家在学校的……边，不远，向……走一公里。

温习 Checkpoint

学生做题前，老师可讲解地图的三要素：比例尺、方向和图例。比例尺用来估算实际距离。有指向标或者经纬网时，可相应确定方向；一般地图则是上北下南，左西右东。图例表示地图上的标记和符号代表了什么事物或地点。在清楚这三要素后，就会容易读懂地图。

1 **Answer the questions to help the children find the way to their destinations.**

1 这是什么车？它向什么方向开？ 这是校车。它向西边开。

2 👄 请问语文中心怎么走？

3 大卫家门口有什么车站？ 大卫家门口有出租车站。

4 大卫家到花园有十公里，很 远 。

5 去大卫家，坐电车还是公共汽车更快？ 去大卫家，坐公共汽车更快。因为这里没有电车，只有公共汽车。

6 活动中心在什么方向？我 要 去那里和同学们一起打球。
活动中心在北方。

评核方法：
学生两人一组，互相考察评价表内单词和句子的听说读写。交际沟通部分由老师朗读要求，
学生再互相对话。如果达到了某项技能要求，则用色笔将星星或小辣椒涂色。

2 Work with your friend. Colour the stars and the chillies.

Words	说	读	写
东	☆	☆	🌶
南	☆	☆	🌶
西	☆	☆	🌶
北	☆	☆	🌶
远	☆	☆	☆
近	☆	☆	☆
校车	☆	☆	🌶
出租车	☆	☆	🌶
更	☆	☆	🌶
要	☆	☆	☆
公里	☆	🌶	🌶

Words and sentences	说	读	写
公共汽车	☆	🌶	🌶
电车	☆	🌶	🌶
语文	☆	🌶	🌶
考试	☆	🌶	🌶
坐公共汽车或电车更快。	☆	☆	🌶
浩浩和玲玲要坐校车回家。	☆	☆	🌶

Say means of transport	☆
Say the directions	☆

3 What does your teacher say?

评核建议：
根据学生课堂表现，分别给予"太棒了！
(Excellent!)"、"不错！(Good!)"或"继续努
力！(Work harder!)"的评价，再让学生圈出
上方对应的表情，以记录自己的学习情况。

My teacher says ...

21

分享 Sharing

延伸活动：
1 学生用手遮盖英文，读中文单词，并思考单词意思；
2 学生用手遮盖中文单词，看着英文说出对应的中文单词；
3 学生三人一组，尽量运用中文单词分角色复述故事。

Words I remember

东	dōng	east
南	nán	south
西	xī	west
北	běi	north
远	yuǎn	far
近	jìn	near
校车	xiào chē	school bus
出租车	chū zū chē	taxi
更	gèng	even more
要	yào	will
公里	gōng lǐ	kilometre (km)
公共汽车	gōng gòng qì chē	bus
电车	diàn chē	tram

Post Office

School

Supermarket

| 语文 | yǔ wén | language |
| 考试 | kǎo shì | examination |

Other words

车站	chē zhàn	station
迷路	mí lù	to lose one's way
向	xiàng	toward
中心	zhōng xīn	center
方向	fāng xiàng	direction
以为	yǐ wéi	to presume, to think
直	zhí	straight
路口	lù kǒu	intersection
转	zhuǎn	to turn
就	jiù	just

OXFORD
UNIVERSITY PRESS

Oxford University Press is a department of the University of Oxford.
It furthers the University's objective of excellence in research, scholarship,
and education by publishing worldwide. Oxford is a registered trade mark of
Oxford University Press in the UK and in certain other countries

Published in Hong Kong by
Oxford University Press (China) Limited
39th Floor, One Kowloon, 1 Wang Yuen Street, Kowloon Bay,
Hong Kong

Illustrated by Anne Lee, Emily Chan, KY Chan and Wildman

Photographs for reproduction permitted by Dreamstime.com

China National Publications Import & Export (Group) Corporation is an authorized distributor of
Oxford Elementary Chinese.

Please contact content@cnpiec.com.cn or 86-10-65856782

ISBN: 978-0-19-047010-4

10 9 8 7 6 5 4 3 2

Teacher's Edition
ISBN: 978-0-19-082318-4

10 9 8 7 6 5 4 3 2